50 Low-Carb Dinner Ideas Recipes for Summer

By: Kelly Johnson

Table of Contents

- Zucchini Noodles with Pesto and Grilled Chicken
- Cauliflower Fried Rice with Shrimp
- Eggplant Lasagna with Ground Turkey
- Stuffed Bell Peppers with Quinoa and Black Beans
- Lemon Garlic Butter Chicken with Asparagus
- Grilled Salmon with Avocado Salsa
- Chicken Alfredo with Spaghetti Squash
- Beef Stir-Fry with Broccoli and Bell Peppers
- Baked Parmesan-Crusted Tilapia
- Lettuce Wrap Tacos with Ground Beef
- Creamy Tuscan Chicken with Spinach and Sun-Dried Tomatoes
- Cabbage Roll Casserole
- Grilled Lemon Herb Chicken Skewers
- Zoodles with Meatballs in Marinara Sauce
- Pork Chops with Mushroom Cream Sauce
- Stuffed Zucchini Boats with Italian Sausage
- Buffalo Cauliflower Bites with Ranch Dressing
- Herb-Crusted Rack of Lamb with Ratatouille
- Chicken Caesar Salad with Homemade Dressing
- Shrimp Tacos with Cabbage Slaw
- Mediterranean Grilled Vegetable Salad
- Pesto Zoodle Salad with Cherry Tomatoes
- Chili-Lime Grilled Chicken Thighs
- Sautéed Spinach with Garlic and Olive Oil
- Roasted Brussels Sprouts with Bacon
- Baked Chicken Drumsticks with Paprika and Garlic
- Broccoli Cheese Casserole
- Egg and Avocado Salad Lettuce Wraps
- Coconut Curry Shrimp with Cauliflower Rice
- Stuffed Mushrooms with Cream Cheese and Bacon

- Grilled Vegetable and Halloumi Skewers
- Savory Cauliflower and Cheese Bake
- Beef and Broccoli Stir-Fry with Almonds
- Creamy Garlic Tuscan Salmon
- Cabbage and Sausage Skillet
- Balsamic Glazed Chicken with Roasted Veggies
- Zucchini and Beef Casserole
- Turkey and Spinach Stuffed Peppers
- Thai Coconut Chicken Soup
- Cilantro Lime Chicken with Avocado Salsa
- Spaghetti Squash with Garlic Butter Shrimp
- Ratatouille with Grilled Chicken
- Oven-Baked Salmon with Lemon-Dill Sauce
- Grilled Chicken and Vegetable Kabobs
- Eggplant Parmesan with Mozzarella Cheese
- Savory Chicken and Vegetable Stir-Fry
- Pork Tenderloin with Garlic and Rosemary
- Roasted Chicken Thighs with Brussels Sprouts
- Egg Drop Soup with Chicken and Vegetables
- Zucchini Fritters with Greek Yogurt Dip

Zucchini Noodles with Pesto and Grilled Chicken

Ingredients

For the Zucchini Noodles:

- 4 medium zucchinis, spiralized
- 1 tablespoon olive oil
- Salt and pepper to taste

For the Pesto:

- 2 cups fresh basil leaves
- 1/2 cup grated Parmesan cheese
- 1/2 cup pine nuts (or walnuts)
- 2 garlic cloves, minced
- 1/2 cup olive oil
- Salt and pepper to taste

For the Grilled Chicken:

- 2 boneless, skinless chicken breasts
- 1 tablespoon olive oil
- Salt and pepper to taste
- 1 teaspoon Italian seasoning (optional)

Instructions

1. Prepare the Pesto:

1. In a food processor, combine basil leaves, Parmesan cheese, pine nuts, and garlic.
2. Pulse until finely chopped.
3. With the processor running, slowly add olive oil until smooth. Season with salt and pepper to taste. Set aside.

2. Grill the Chicken:

1. Preheat the grill to medium-high heat.
2. Brush the chicken breasts with olive oil and season with salt, pepper, and Italian seasoning (if using).

3. Grill the chicken for about 6-7 minutes on each side or until the internal temperature reaches 165°F (75°C). Remove from the grill and let it rest before slicing.

3. Cook the Zucchini Noodles:

1. In a large skillet, heat olive oil over medium heat.
2. Add the spiralized zucchini noodles and sauté for about 3-4 minutes until just tender. Season with salt and pepper.

4. Assemble the Dish:

1. Toss the cooked zucchini noodles with the pesto until evenly coated.
2. Serve the zucchini noodles topped with sliced grilled chicken.

Tips:

- For added flavor, consider adding cherry tomatoes or spinach to the zucchini noodles.
- You can also use store-bought pesto if you're short on time.

Enjoy your healthy and flavorful **Zucchini Noodles with Pesto and Grilled Chicken**!

Cauliflower Fried Rice with Shrimp

Ingredients

- 1 medium head of cauliflower, grated or processed into rice
- 1 lb shrimp, peeled and deveined
- 2 tablespoons sesame oil
- 1 cup mixed vegetables (carrots, peas, bell peppers)
- 3 green onions, chopped
- 2 cloves garlic, minced
- 2 tablespoons soy sauce (or tamari for gluten-free)
- Salt and pepper to taste
- 2 eggs, lightly beaten (optional)

Instructions

1. Heat 1 tablespoon of sesame oil in a large skillet over medium heat. Add shrimp and cook until pink, about 2-3 minutes. Remove and set aside.
2. In the same skillet, add the remaining oil and garlic. Sauté for 30 seconds.
3. Add cauliflower rice and mixed vegetables. Stir-fry for 5-7 minutes until tender.
4. Push the rice to one side, pour in the beaten eggs (if using), and scramble them until cooked.
5. Add shrimp back into the skillet along with soy sauce, green onions, salt, and pepper. Mix well and serve hot.

Eggplant Lasagna with Ground Turkey

Ingredients

- 2 medium eggplants, sliced lengthwise
- 1 lb ground turkey
- 2 cups marinara sauce
- 1 cup ricotta cheese
- 1 cup shredded mozzarella cheese
- 1/2 cup grated Parmesan cheese
- 2 tablespoons olive oil
- Salt and pepper to taste
- Italian seasoning (optional)

Instructions

1. Preheat the oven to 375°F (190°C).
2. Brush eggplant slices with olive oil and sprinkle with salt. Place on a baking sheet and bake for 15-20 minutes until slightly softened.
3. In a skillet, cook ground turkey over medium heat until browned. Drain excess fat and stir in marinara sauce. Simmer for 5 minutes.
4. In a baking dish, layer eggplant slices, ricotta cheese, turkey mixture, and mozzarella cheese. Repeat layers, finishing with mozzarella and Parmesan on top.
5. Bake for 25-30 minutes until cheese is bubbly and golden. Let cool slightly before slicing.

Stuffed Bell Peppers with Quinoa and Black Beans

Ingredients

- 4 bell peppers (any color)
- 1 cup cooked quinoa
- 1 can black beans, rinsed and drained
- 1 cup corn (fresh or frozen)
- 1 teaspoon cumin
- 1 teaspoon chili powder
- Salt and pepper to taste
- 1 cup salsa
- 1 cup shredded cheese (optional)

Instructions

1. Preheat the oven to 375°F (190°C).
2. Cut the tops off the bell peppers and remove seeds. Place them in a baking dish.
3. In a bowl, mix quinoa, black beans, corn, cumin, chili powder, salt, and pepper. Stir in salsa.
4. Fill each pepper with the quinoa mixture and top with cheese if desired.
5. Bake for 25-30 minutes until peppers are tender. Serve warm.

Let me know if you need anything else!

Lemon Garlic Butter Chicken with Asparagus

Ingredients

- 4 boneless, skinless chicken breasts
- 2 tablespoons butter
- 3 cloves garlic, minced
- 1 lemon, juiced and zested
- 1 lb asparagus, trimmed
- Salt and pepper to taste
- Fresh parsley, chopped (for garnish)

Instructions

1. Preheat the oven to 400°F (200°C).
2. In a large oven-safe skillet, melt butter over medium heat. Add garlic and sauté until fragrant.
3. Season chicken breasts with salt and pepper, then add them to the skillet, cooking for about 5 minutes on each side until golden.
4. Add lemon juice, zest, and asparagus to the skillet. Toss to coat.
5. Transfer the skillet to the oven and bake for 15-20 minutes until chicken is cooked through. Garnish with parsley before serving.

Grilled Salmon with Avocado Salsa

Ingredients

- 4 salmon fillets
- 2 tablespoons olive oil
- Salt and pepper to taste
- 1 avocado, diced
- 1 tomato, diced
- 1/4 red onion, finely chopped
- Juice of 1 lime
- Fresh cilantro, chopped (optional)

Instructions

1. Preheat the grill to medium-high heat. Brush salmon fillets with olive oil and season with salt and pepper.
2. Grill salmon for 4-5 minutes per side, until cooked through.
3. In a bowl, combine avocado, tomato, onion, lime juice, and cilantro. Mix gently.
4. Serve grilled salmon topped with avocado salsa.

Chicken Alfredo with Spaghetti Squash

Ingredients

- 1 medium spaghetti squash
- 2 cups cooked, shredded chicken
- 1 cup heavy cream
- 1/2 cup grated Parmesan cheese
- 3 cloves garlic, minced
- Salt and pepper to taste
- Fresh parsley, chopped (for garnish)

Instructions

1. Preheat the oven to 400°F (200°C). Cut spaghetti squash in half, remove seeds, and place cut-side down on a baking sheet. Bake for 30-40 minutes until tender.
2. In a saucepan, heat heavy cream over medium heat. Add garlic, salt, pepper, and Parmesan cheese, stirring until combined.
3. Once spaghetti squash is done, use a fork to scrape out the strands.
4. Combine squash with shredded chicken and Alfredo sauce. Serve garnished with parsley.

Beef Stir-Fry with Broccoli and Bell Peppers

Ingredients

- 1 lb beef sirloin, sliced thinly
- 2 cups broccoli florets
- 1 bell pepper, sliced
- 2 tablespoons soy sauce
- 2 tablespoons sesame oil
- 3 cloves garlic, minced
- 1 teaspoon ginger, grated
- Cooked rice (for serving)

Instructions

1. Heat sesame oil in a large skillet over medium-high heat. Add beef and cook until browned. Remove from skillet.
2. In the same skillet, add broccoli, bell pepper, garlic, and ginger. Stir-fry for 3-4 minutes until vegetables are tender-crisp.
3. Return beef to the skillet, add soy sauce, and stir until heated through. Serve over cooked rice.

Baked Parmesan-Crusted Tilapia

Ingredients

- 4 tilapia fillets
- 1/2 cup grated Parmesan cheese
- 1/2 cup breadcrumbs
- 2 tablespoons melted butter
- 1 teaspoon garlic powder
- Salt and pepper to taste

Instructions

1. Preheat the oven to 400°F (200°C).
2. In a bowl, combine Parmesan cheese, breadcrumbs, garlic powder, salt, and pepper.
3. Brush tilapia fillets with melted butter, then coat with the breadcrumb mixture.
4. Place on a baking sheet and bake for 15-20 minutes until the fish is cooked through and flaky.

Lettuce Wrap Tacos with Ground Beef

Ingredients

- 1 lb ground beef
- 1 packet taco seasoning
- 1 head of lettuce (like butter or iceberg)
- Diced tomatoes, cheese, and avocado (for toppings)

Instructions

1. In a skillet, brown ground beef over medium heat. Drain excess fat.
2. Add taco seasoning and follow package instructions.
3. Use lettuce leaves as wraps and fill with seasoned beef. Top with tomatoes, cheese, and avocado.

Creamy Tuscan Chicken with Spinach and Sun-Dried Tomatoes

Ingredients

- 4 boneless, skinless chicken breasts
- 2 cups fresh spinach
- 1/2 cup sun-dried tomatoes, chopped
- 1 cup heavy cream
- 1/2 cup grated Parmesan cheese
- 2 tablespoons olive oil
- Salt and pepper to taste

Instructions

1. Heat olive oil in a skillet over medium heat. Season chicken with salt and pepper, and cook until browned and cooked through. Remove from skillet.
2. In the same skillet, add sun-dried tomatoes and spinach. Cook until spinach wilts.
3. Add heavy cream and Parmesan, stirring until sauce thickens. Return chicken to skillet to coat in sauce. Serve warm.

Let me know if you need any adjustments!

Cabbage Roll Casserole

Ingredients

- 1 head of cabbage, chopped
- 1 lb ground beef or turkey
- 1 cup cooked rice
- 1 can (15 oz) tomato sauce
- 1 can (14.5 oz) diced tomatoes
- 1 onion, chopped
- 2 cloves garlic, minced
- 1 teaspoon paprika
- Salt and pepper to taste

Instructions

1. Preheat the oven to 350°F (175°C).
2. In a large skillet, sauté onion and garlic until translucent. Add ground meat and cook until browned.
3. Stir in cooked rice, tomato sauce, diced tomatoes, paprika, salt, and pepper.
4. In a greased baking dish, layer half the cabbage, then the meat mixture, and top with remaining cabbage.
5. Cover with foil and bake for 45 minutes. Remove foil and bake for an additional 15 minutes.

Grilled Lemon Herb Chicken Skewers

Ingredients

- 1 lb chicken breast, cut into cubes
- 1/4 cup olive oil
- Juice of 2 lemons
- 2 cloves garlic, minced
- 1 tablespoon dried oregano
- Salt and pepper to taste
- Skewers (wooden or metal)

Instructions

1. In a bowl, whisk together olive oil, lemon juice, garlic, oregano, salt, and pepper.
2. Add chicken cubes to the marinade and let sit for at least 30 minutes.
3. Preheat the grill to medium-high heat. Thread chicken onto skewers.
4. Grill skewers for 10-12 minutes, turning occasionally, until cooked through.

Zoodles with Meatballs in Marinara Sauce

Ingredients

- 2 medium zucchinis, spiralized
- 1 lb ground beef or turkey
- 1/2 cup breadcrumbs
- 1 egg
- 2 cups marinara sauce
- 1/2 teaspoon Italian seasoning
- Salt and pepper to taste

Instructions

1. In a bowl, mix ground meat, breadcrumbs, egg, Italian seasoning, salt, and pepper. Form into meatballs.
2. In a skillet, cook meatballs over medium heat until browned on all sides.
3. Add marinara sauce to the skillet and simmer for 10-15 minutes.
4. In another skillet, sauté zoodles for 2-3 minutes until just tender. Serve meatballs and sauce over zoodles.

Pork Chops with Mushroom Cream Sauce

Ingredients

- 4 pork chops
- 2 tablespoons olive oil
- 1 cup mushrooms, sliced
- 1 cup heavy cream
- 1 teaspoon garlic powder
- Salt and pepper to taste

Instructions

1. Heat olive oil in a skillet over medium-high heat. Season pork chops with salt and pepper.
2. Cook pork chops for 4-5 minutes on each side until cooked through. Remove from skillet.
3. In the same skillet, add mushrooms and sauté until browned.
4. Stir in heavy cream and garlic powder, cooking until the sauce thickens. Pour over pork chops before serving.

Stuffed Zucchini Boats with Italian Sausage

Ingredients

- 4 medium zucchinis, halved and hollowed
- 1 lb Italian sausage, removed from casings
- 1 cup marinara sauce
- 1 cup shredded mozzarella cheese
- 1/4 cup grated Parmesan cheese

Instructions

1. Preheat the oven to 375°F (190°C).
2. In a skillet, cook Italian sausage until browned. Stir in marinara sauce and simmer for 5 minutes.
3. Fill zucchini halves with sausage mixture and place in a baking dish.
4. Top with mozzarella and Parmesan cheese. Bake for 20-25 minutes until zucchini is tender.

Buffalo Cauliflower Bites with Ranch Dressing

Ingredients

- 1 head of cauliflower, cut into florets
- 1/2 cup buffalo sauce
- 1/2 cup breadcrumbs
- 1/4 cup grated Parmesan cheese
- Ranch dressing (for serving)

Instructions

1. Preheat the oven to 450°F (230°C).
2. In a bowl, toss cauliflower florets with buffalo sauce.
3. In another bowl, mix breadcrumbs and Parmesan cheese.
4. Coat buffalo cauliflower in the breadcrumb mixture and place on a baking sheet.
5. Bake for 20-25 minutes until crispy. Serve with ranch dressing.

Herb-Crusted Rack of Lamb with Ratatouille

Ingredients

- 1 rack of lamb, frenched
- 2 tablespoons Dijon mustard
- 1 cup breadcrumbs
- 1/4 cup fresh herbs (rosemary, thyme, parsley), chopped
- Salt and pepper to taste
- 2 cups ratatouille (zucchini, eggplant, bell peppers, tomatoes)

Instructions

1. Preheat the oven to 400°F (200°C).
2. Season rack of lamb with salt and pepper. Brush with Dijon mustard.
3. In a bowl, mix breadcrumbs and herbs. Coat the lamb with the breadcrumb mixture.
4. Place on a baking sheet and roast for 25-30 minutes for medium-rare. Let rest before slicing.
5. Serve with ratatouille on the side.

Let me know if you need any further adjustments!

Chicken Caesar Salad with Homemade Dressing

Ingredients

- 2 chicken breasts, grilled and sliced
- 4 cups romaine lettuce, chopped
- 1/2 cup croutons
- 1/4 cup grated Parmesan cheese
- 1/4 cup mayonnaise
- 2 tablespoons lemon juice
- 1 tablespoon Dijon mustard
- 1 clove garlic, minced
- Salt and pepper to taste

Instructions

1. In a bowl, whisk together mayonnaise, lemon juice, Dijon mustard, garlic, salt, and pepper to make the dressing.
2. In a large bowl, combine lettuce, grilled chicken, croutons, and Parmesan cheese.
3. Drizzle dressing over the salad and toss gently to combine. Serve immediately.

Shrimp Tacos with Cabbage Slaw

Ingredients

- 1 lb shrimp, peeled and deveined
- 1 tablespoon olive oil
- 1 teaspoon chili powder
- Salt and pepper to taste
- 8 small corn tortillas
- 2 cups green cabbage, shredded
- 1/4 cup cilantro, chopped
- 1 lime, juiced

Instructions

1. In a skillet, heat olive oil over medium heat. Season shrimp with chili powder, salt, and pepper, then cook for 2-3 minutes per side until pink and cooked through.
2. In a bowl, mix cabbage, cilantro, and lime juice.
3. Warm tortillas and fill each with shrimp and cabbage slaw. Serve with lime wedges.

Mediterranean Grilled Vegetable Salad

Ingredients

- 1 zucchini, sliced
- 1 bell pepper, sliced
- 1 eggplant, cubed
- 1 cup cherry tomatoes, halved
- 1/4 cup olive oil
- 2 tablespoons balsamic vinegar
- Salt and pepper to taste
- 1/4 cup feta cheese, crumbled

Instructions

1. Preheat the grill to medium-high heat. Toss vegetables with olive oil, balsamic vinegar, salt, and pepper.
2. Grill vegetables for 8-10 minutes until tender and slightly charred.
3. Let cool slightly, then toss with feta cheese before serving.

Pesto Zoodle Salad with Cherry Tomatoes

Ingredients

- 2 medium zucchinis, spiralized
- 1 cup cherry tomatoes, halved
- 1/4 cup basil pesto
- 1/4 cup grated Parmesan cheese
- Salt and pepper to taste

Instructions

1. In a bowl, combine spiralized zucchini, cherry tomatoes, pesto, and Parmesan cheese.
2. Toss to coat the zoodles evenly with pesto. Season with salt and pepper to taste.
3. Serve chilled or at room temperature.

Chili-Lime Grilled Chicken Thighs

Ingredients

- 4 chicken thighs, bone-in and skin-on
- 1/4 cup olive oil
- Juice of 2 limes
- 1 teaspoon chili powder
- 1 teaspoon cumin
- Salt and pepper to taste

Instructions

1. In a bowl, mix olive oil, lime juice, chili powder, cumin, salt, and pepper.
2. Marinate chicken thighs in the mixture for at least 30 minutes.
3. Preheat the grill to medium-high heat and cook chicken for 6-7 minutes per side until cooked through.

Sautéed Spinach with Garlic and Olive Oil

Ingredients

- 2 tablespoons olive oil
- 3 cloves garlic, minced
- 8 cups fresh spinach
- Salt and pepper to taste

Instructions

1. In a skillet, heat olive oil over medium heat. Add garlic and sauté until fragrant.
2. Add spinach and cook until wilted, about 3-4 minutes.
3. Season with salt and pepper before serving.

Roasted Brussels Sprouts with Bacon

Ingredients

- 1 lb Brussels sprouts, halved
- 4 slices bacon, chopped
- 2 tablespoons olive oil
- Salt and pepper to taste

Instructions

1. Preheat the oven to 400°F (200°C).
2. In a baking dish, toss Brussels sprouts with bacon, olive oil, salt, and pepper.
3. Roast for 20-25 minutes until sprouts are tender and bacon is crispy.

Let me know if you need any more adjustments!

Baked Chicken Drumsticks with Paprika and Garlic

Ingredients

- 8 chicken drumsticks
- 2 tablespoons olive oil
- 1 tablespoon paprika
- 1 teaspoon garlic powder
- Salt and pepper to taste

Instructions

1. Preheat the oven to 425°F (220°C).
2. In a bowl, mix olive oil, paprika, garlic powder, salt, and pepper.
3. Toss chicken drumsticks in the mixture until well coated and place on a baking sheet.
4. Bake for 35-40 minutes, turning halfway through, until the chicken is cooked through and crispy.

Broccoli Cheese Casserole

Ingredients

- 4 cups broccoli florets, steamed
- 1 cup cheddar cheese, shredded
- 1/2 cup mayonnaise
- 1/2 cup sour cream
- 1 teaspoon garlic powder
- 1/2 cup breadcrumbs

Instructions

1. Preheat the oven to 350°F (175°C).
2. In a bowl, mix steamed broccoli, cheddar cheese, mayonnaise, sour cream, and garlic powder.
3. Transfer to a greased baking dish and top with breadcrumbs.
4. Bake for 25-30 minutes until bubbly and golden on top.

Egg and Avocado Salad Lettuce Wraps

Ingredients

- 4 hard-boiled eggs, chopped
- 1 avocado, mashed
- 2 tablespoons Greek yogurt
- 1 tablespoon lemon juice
- Salt and pepper to taste
- Lettuce leaves for wrapping

Instructions

1. In a bowl, combine chopped eggs, mashed avocado, Greek yogurt, lemon juice, salt, and pepper.
2. Mix until well combined.
3. Spoon the mixture onto lettuce leaves and serve as wraps.

Coconut Curry Shrimp with Cauliflower Rice

Ingredients

- 1 lb shrimp, peeled and deveined
- 1 can (14 oz) coconut milk
- 2 tablespoons curry powder
- 1 cup cauliflower rice
- 1 tablespoon olive oil
- Salt to taste

Instructions

1. In a skillet, heat olive oil over medium heat. Add shrimp and cook until pink, about 2-3 minutes.
2. Stir in coconut milk and curry powder, and simmer for 5-7 minutes.
3. In another pan, sauté cauliflower rice until tender. Serve shrimp over cauliflower rice.

Stuffed Mushrooms with Cream Cheese and Bacon

Ingredients

- 12 large mushrooms, stems removed
- 4 oz cream cheese, softened
- 4 slices bacon, cooked and crumbled
- 1/4 cup green onions, chopped
- 1/4 teaspoon garlic powder

Instructions

1. Preheat the oven to 375°F (190°C).
2. In a bowl, mix cream cheese, crumbled bacon, green onions, and garlic powder.
3. Fill each mushroom cap with the cream cheese mixture and place on a baking sheet.
4. Bake for 15-20 minutes until mushrooms are tender and filling is bubbly.

Grilled Vegetable and Halloumi Skewers

Ingredients

- 1 block halloumi cheese, cut into cubes
- 1 zucchini, sliced
- 1 bell pepper, chopped
- 1 red onion, chopped
- 2 tablespoons olive oil
- Salt and pepper to taste

Instructions

1. Preheat the grill to medium-high heat.
2. Thread halloumi, zucchini, bell pepper, and red onion onto skewers. Drizzle with olive oil and season with salt and pepper.
3. Grill skewers for 8-10 minutes, turning occasionally until vegetables are tender and halloumi is golden.

Savory Cauliflower and Cheese Bake

Ingredients

- 1 head of cauliflower, cut into florets
- 1 cup cheddar cheese, shredded
- 1/2 cup milk
- 2 tablespoons butter
- 1/4 cup breadcrumbs
- Salt and pepper to taste

Instructions

1. Preheat the oven to 375°F (190°C).
2. Boil cauliflower florets until tender, about 5-7 minutes. Drain and place in a baking dish.
3. In a saucepan, melt butter and stir in milk, cheese, salt, and pepper until cheese is melted.
4. Pour cheese sauce over cauliflower, top with breadcrumbs, and bake for 20-25 minutes until bubbly and golden.

Let me know if you need any more changes!

Beef and Broccoli Stir-Fry with Almonds

Ingredients

- 1 lb beef sirloin, thinly sliced
- 4 cups broccoli florets
- 1/4 cup soy sauce
- 2 tablespoons sesame oil
- 2 cloves garlic, minced
- 1/4 cup sliced almonds

Instructions

1. In a skillet, heat sesame oil over medium-high heat. Add sliced beef and cook until browned, about 3-4 minutes.
2. Add garlic and broccoli, stirring to combine. Pour in soy sauce and cook for another 5 minutes until broccoli is tender.
3. Top with sliced almonds before serving.

Creamy Garlic Tuscan Salmon

Ingredients

- 4 salmon fillets
- 2 tablespoons olive oil
- 4 cloves garlic, minced
- 1 cup heavy cream
- 1 cup spinach
- 1/2 cup sun-dried tomatoes, chopped

Instructions

1. In a skillet, heat olive oil over medium heat. Add salmon fillets and cook for 4-5 minutes per side until cooked through. Remove and set aside.
2. In the same skillet, add garlic and sauté until fragrant. Stir in heavy cream, spinach, and sun-dried tomatoes, cooking until spinach wilts.
3. Return salmon to the skillet and coat with the creamy sauce before serving.

Cabbage and Sausage Skillet

Ingredients

- 1 lb smoked sausage, sliced
- 4 cups green cabbage, chopped
- 1 onion, sliced
- 2 tablespoons olive oil
- Salt and pepper to taste

Instructions

1. In a large skillet, heat olive oil over medium heat. Add sausage and cook until browned, about 5 minutes.
2. Stir in onion and cabbage, cooking until cabbage is wilted and tender, about 10-12 minutes.
3. Season with salt and pepper before serving.

Balsamic Glazed Chicken with Roasted Veggies

Ingredients

- 4 chicken breasts
- 1/2 cup balsamic vinegar
- 2 tablespoons honey
- 2 cups mixed vegetables (bell peppers, zucchini, carrots)
- 2 tablespoons olive oil

Instructions

1. Preheat the oven to 400°F (200°C).
2. In a bowl, mix balsamic vinegar and honey. Place chicken in a baking dish and pour glaze over it.
3. Toss vegetables with olive oil, salt, and pepper, and arrange around chicken. Bake for 25-30 minutes until chicken is cooked through and veggies are tender.

Zucchini and Beef Casserole

Ingredients

- 1 lb ground beef
- 2 zucchinis, sliced
- 1 can (14 oz) diced tomatoes
- 1 cup shredded cheese
- 1 teaspoon Italian seasoning

Instructions

1. Preheat the oven to 350°F (175°C).
2. In a skillet, brown ground beef over medium heat. Drain excess fat and stir in diced tomatoes and Italian seasoning.
3. In a baking dish, layer zucchini slices and beef mixture, topping with cheese. Bake for 20-25 minutes until cheese is melted and bubbly.

Turkey and Spinach Stuffed Peppers

Ingredients

- 4 bell peppers, halved and seeded
- 1 lb ground turkey
- 2 cups spinach, chopped
- 1 cup cooked quinoa
- 1 cup marinara sauce

Instructions

1. Preheat the oven to 375°F (190°C).
2. In a skillet, cook ground turkey until browned. Stir in spinach, cooked quinoa, and marinara sauce until heated through.
3. Stuff bell pepper halves with the turkey mixture and place in a baking dish. Bake for 25-30 minutes until peppers are tender.

Thai Coconut Chicken Soup

Ingredients

- 1 lb chicken breast, sliced
- 1 can (14 oz) coconut milk
- 4 cups chicken broth
- 1 tablespoon red curry paste
- 1 cup mushrooms, sliced
- Juice of 1 lime

Instructions

1. In a pot, combine chicken broth, coconut milk, and red curry paste. Bring to a simmer.
2. Add chicken and mushrooms, cooking until chicken is cooked through, about 10-15 minutes.
3. Stir in lime juice before serving.

Let me know if you need any more adjustments!

Cilantro Lime Chicken with Avocado Salsa

Ingredients

- 4 chicken breasts
- 1/4 cup lime juice
- 1/4 cup cilantro, chopped
- 1 avocado, diced
- 1 tomato, diced
- Salt and pepper to taste

Instructions

1. In a bowl, combine lime juice, cilantro, salt, and pepper. Marinate chicken breasts in the mixture for at least 30 minutes.
2. Grill chicken over medium heat for 6-7 minutes per side until cooked through.
3. In another bowl, mix avocado, tomato, and a bit of lime juice. Serve the chicken topped with avocado salsa.

Spaghetti Squash with Garlic Butter Shrimp

Ingredients

- 1 spaghetti squash
- 1 lb shrimp, peeled and deveined
- 4 cloves garlic, minced
- 4 tablespoons butter
- Salt and pepper to taste

Instructions

1. Preheat the oven to 400°F (200°C). Cut the spaghetti squash in half, remove seeds, and place cut-side down on a baking sheet. Bake for 40-45 minutes until tender.
2. In a skillet, melt butter over medium heat. Add garlic and shrimp, cooking until shrimp is pink, about 3-4 minutes.
3. Scrape the spaghetti squash with a fork to create strands and toss with the shrimp and garlic butter before serving.

Ratatouille with Grilled Chicken

Ingredients

- 2 zucchinis, sliced
- 1 eggplant, diced
- 1 bell pepper, chopped
- 1 can (14 oz) diced tomatoes
- 2 chicken breasts, grilled and sliced

Instructions

1. In a large skillet, sauté zucchini, eggplant, and bell pepper until tender.
2. Stir in diced tomatoes and cook for another 5 minutes.
3. Serve ratatouille topped with sliced grilled chicken.

Oven-Baked Salmon with Lemon-Dill Sauce

Ingredients

- 4 salmon fillets
- 2 tablespoons olive oil
- 1 lemon, zested and juiced
- 2 tablespoons fresh dill, chopped
- Salt and pepper to taste

Instructions

1. Preheat the oven to 375°F (190°C).
2. In a bowl, mix olive oil, lemon juice, zest, dill, salt, and pepper.
3. Place salmon on a baking sheet and brush with the lemon-dill mixture. Bake for 15-20 minutes until salmon is cooked through.

Grilled Chicken and Vegetable Kabobs

Ingredients

- 2 chicken breasts, cubed
- 1 bell pepper, chopped
- 1 zucchini, sliced
- 1 onion, chopped
- 1/4 cup olive oil
- Salt and pepper to taste

Instructions

1. Preheat the grill to medium-high heat.
2. In a bowl, combine chicken, bell pepper, zucchini, onion, olive oil, salt, and pepper. Thread onto skewers.
3. Grill kabobs for 10-12 minutes, turning occasionally until chicken is cooked through.

Eggplant Parmesan with Mozzarella Cheese

Ingredients

- 2 eggplants, sliced
- 2 cups marinara sauce
- 2 cups mozzarella cheese, shredded
- 1/2 cup Parmesan cheese, grated
- 1/4 cup breadcrumbs

Instructions

1. Preheat the oven to 375°F (190°C).
2. Layer eggplant slices in a baking dish, topping each layer with marinara sauce, mozzarella, and Parmesan cheese.
3. Sprinkle breadcrumbs on top and bake for 30-35 minutes until golden and bubbly.

Let me know if you need any more adjustments!

Savory Chicken and Vegetable Stir-Fry

Ingredients

- 1 lb chicken breast, sliced
- 2 cups mixed vegetables (bell peppers, broccoli, snap peas)
- 2 tablespoons soy sauce
- 1 tablespoon sesame oil
- 2 cloves garlic, minced

Instructions

1. In a large skillet, heat sesame oil over medium-high heat. Add sliced chicken and cook until browned, about 5-7 minutes.
2. Add garlic and mixed vegetables, stirring to combine. Pour in soy sauce and cook for another 5 minutes until vegetables are tender.
3. Serve hot over rice or noodles.

Pork Tenderloin with Garlic and Rosemary

Ingredients

- 1 lb pork tenderloin
- 3 cloves garlic, minced
- 2 tablespoons fresh rosemary, chopped
- 2 tablespoons olive oil
- Salt and pepper to taste

Instructions

1. Preheat the oven to 400°F (200°C).
2. In a bowl, mix garlic, rosemary, olive oil, salt, and pepper. Rub the mixture over the pork tenderloin.
3. Place the pork in a baking dish and roast for 25-30 minutes until cooked through. Let rest before slicing.

Roasted Chicken Thighs with Brussels Sprouts

Ingredients

- 4 chicken thighs, bone-in and skin-on
- 2 cups Brussels sprouts, halved
- 2 tablespoons olive oil
- Salt and pepper to taste

Instructions

1. Preheat the oven to 425°F (220°C).
2. In a bowl, toss Brussels sprouts with olive oil, salt, and pepper. Arrange in a baking dish.
3. Place chicken thighs on top and roast for 35-40 minutes until chicken is cooked through and Brussels sprouts are tender.

Egg Drop Soup with Chicken and Vegetables

Ingredients

- 4 cups chicken broth
- 1 cup cooked chicken, shredded
- 2 eggs, beaten
- 1 cup mixed vegetables (carrots, peas)
- 1 tablespoon soy sauce

Instructions

1. In a pot, bring chicken broth to a boil. Add cooked chicken and mixed vegetables.
2. Slowly drizzle in beaten eggs while stirring to create egg ribbons.
3. Stir in soy sauce and serve hot.

Zucchini Fritters with Greek Yogurt Dip

Ingredients

- 2 zucchinis, grated
- 1 egg, beaten
- 1/4 cup flour
- 1/2 cup feta cheese, crumbled
- 1 cup Greek yogurt
- 1 tablespoon lemon juice

Instructions

1. In a bowl, mix grated zucchini, egg, flour, and feta cheese. Form into patties.
2. In a skillet, heat oil over medium heat and cook fritters for 3-4 minutes per side until golden brown.
3. For the dip, mix Greek yogurt with lemon juice and serve alongside fritters.

Let me know if you need any more adjustments!

www.ingramcontent.com/pod-product-compliance
Lightning Source LLC
LaVergne TN
LVHW061950070526
838199LV00060B/4066